Simple Machines
SPRINGS

David Glover

Heinemann Library
Chicago, Illinois

Customer Service 888-454-2279
Visit our website at www.heinemannraintree.com

Designed by Victoria Bevan and Q2A Creative
Illustrations by Barry Atkinson (pp. 9, 17) and Tony Kenyon (pp. 7, 13, 21)
Printed in China by Leo Paper Group

14 13
10 9 8 7 6 5 4

New edition ISBN: 1-4034-8567-4 (hardback)
                            1-4034-8596-8 (paperback)

The Library of Congress has cataloged the first edition as follows:
Glover, David, 1953 Sept. 4-
      Springs / David Glover.
          p.   cm. -- (Simple Machines)
      Includes index.
      Summary: Introduces the principles of springs as simple machines, using examples from
everyday life.
      ISBN 1-57572-082-5 (lib. bdg.)
      1. Springs (Mechanism) - Juvenile literature. [1. Springs (Mechanism)] I. Title. II. Series:
Glover, David, 1953 Sept. 4– Simple Machines.
TJ210.G55 1997
621.8' 11—dc20
                                                                                                      96-15799
                                                                                                              CIP
                                                                                                              AC

Acknowledgments
The author and publishers are grateful to the following for permission to reproduce photographs:
Trevor Clifford pp. 3, 4, 5, 6, 9, 10, 12, 13, 15, 18, 19, 20, 21, 22, 23; Sealy p. 8; Spectrum Colour Library
p. 14; Stockfile/Steven Behr p. 16; Zefa p. 17.

Cover reproduced with permission of Corbis.

The publishers would like to thank Angela Royston for her assistance in the preparation of this edition.

Every effort has been made to contact copyright holders of any material reproduced in this book.
Any omissions will be rectified in subsequent printings if notice is given to the publisher.

The paper used to print this book comes from sustainable sources.

Contents

Some words are shown in bold, **like this**. You can find the definitions for these words in the glossary.

What Are Springs?

Most springs are made from metal wire or strips. If you squeeze a spring, stretch it, bend it, or wind it up, it always tries to spring back into shape.

This jack-in-a-box is a spring toy. When you push the jack down into the box and fasten the lid, you are squeezing the spring.

When you unfasten the lid, the spring makes the jack jump from its box. It can make you jump with surprise!

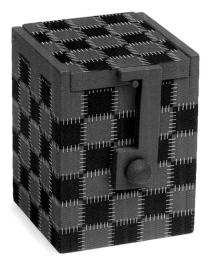

Working springs

Springs store up the work you do when you make them change shape. When you let go of a squeezed spring, it uses the stored work to make things move.

Pogo Stick

A pogo stick has a strong spring that bounces you up in the air. A rubber foot stops the stick from slipping on the ground.

 **FACT FILE** **Pogo crazy**

In 1999 Ashrita Furman used a pogo stick to jump up the 1,899 steps of the CN Tower in Ontario, Canada.

The spring on a pogo stick is a strong **spiral** of steel wire. Your weight pushes it down to make it shorter. The spring pushes back up as it tries to return to its normal shape. This force lifts you up into the air.

When you jump with a pogo stick, you push down the spring.

The spring pushes back up and bounces you into the air.

When you land, the spring is pushed down again, ready for the next bounce.

Spring Beds and Chairs

Have you ever bounced on your bed? Many bed mattresses are filled with wire springs. These help you to sleep comfortably at night. When you lie on the bed, the squeezed springs support every part of your body.

The springs on this chair make the seat soft and comfortable. When you sit on this chair, the springs stretch to hold up your weight.

Spring words

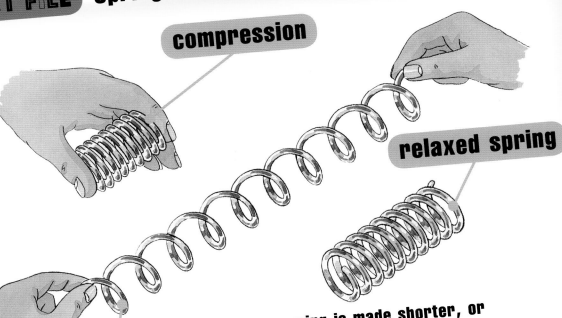

compression

relaxed spring

tension

When a spring is made shorter, or squeezed, we say that it is compressed. When a spring is made longer, or stretched, we say that it is in tension.

Door Springs and Locks

This gate has a spring at the top. It pulls the gate shut when someone leaves it open.

This door has a spring at the bottom. It stops the door from banging against the wall when someone pushes it open too hard.

The door handle below has a spring inside. When you turn the handle, it pulls back the **catch**. When you let go of the handle, the spring pushes the catch back into place.

The door spring and the catch spring work together to keep the door shut.

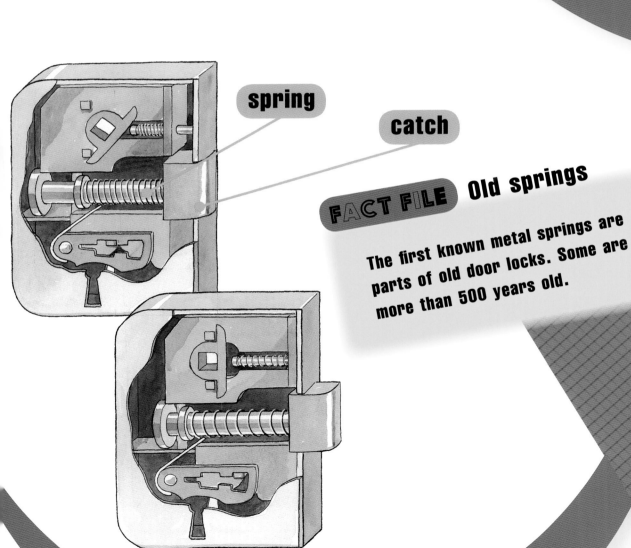

spring

catch

FACT FILE Old springs

The first known metal springs are parts of old door locks. Some are more than 500 years old.

Spring Loaded

This pen has a spring inside it. We say that the pen is **spring loaded**. When you press the button at the bottom, the pen tip comes out of the case. A spring tries to push the tip back inside, but a **catch** holds it in place. When you press the button again, this releases the catch, and the tip goes back inside the pen case.

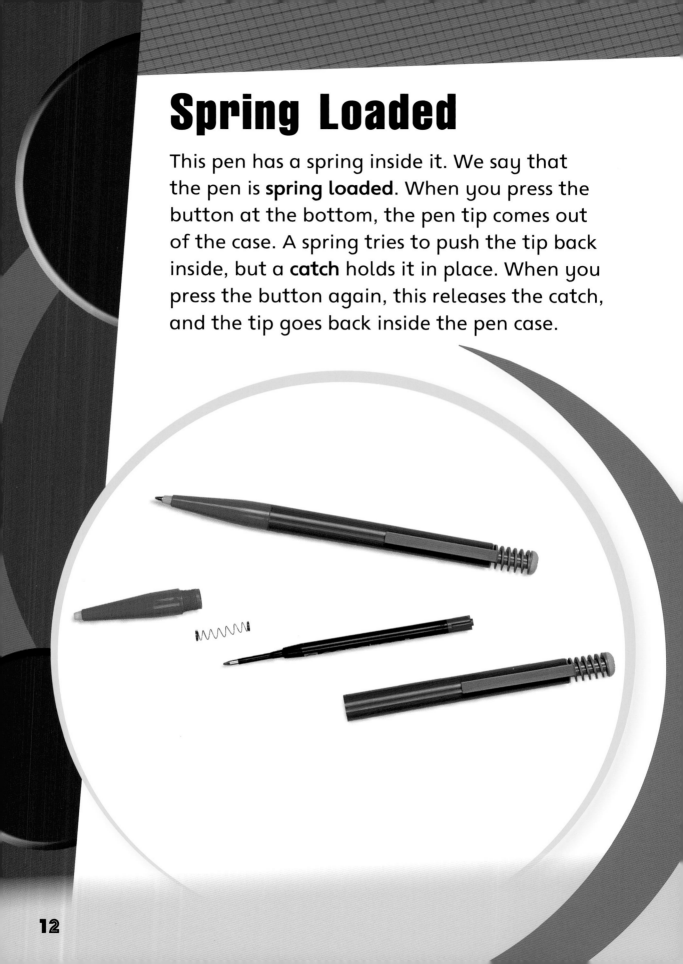

Spring-loaded umbrellas are handy for carrying in a small bag. When it rains, you take off the cover and release the catch, and the umbrella then springs open. A squeezed spring inside the handle does all the **work** for you.

Springy hats!

In the 1800s, some men wore spring loaded top hats. At the theater, they flattened their tall hats under the seats. When the play was over, they let the hats spring back into shape.

13

Spring Balances

A spring balance is a simple weighing machine that uses a spring. Fishermen often use spring balances to weigh their fish.

The weight of the fish stretches the spring. The stretched spring turns a needle around a **dial**. The heavier the fish, the more the spring stretches and the farther the needle turns.

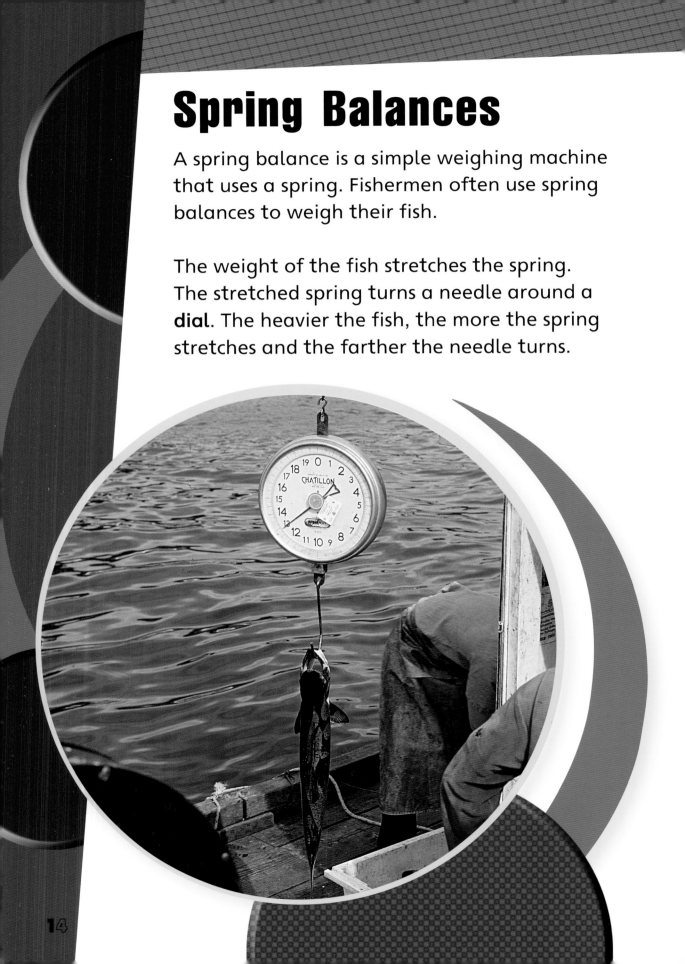

Some bathroom scales have a stiff spring inside. When you stand on the scale, the spring inside stretches a small amount. This small movement is **magnified** by **levers**. The levers turn a dial to show your weight.

Spring Wheels

Some mountain bikes have springs in their **forks**. The springs squeeze and stretch when the wheels go over bumps and holes. This makes the ride more comfortable and lets you go faster.

Motocross bikes speed around a very rough course. They leap high in the air over the hills and hit the ground again with a jolt. Their long springs help to soften the landing for the rider.

FACT FILE Carriage springs

Special sets of springs were invented for horse-drawn carriages. They helped to make the passengers comfortable. The springs were made from thin strips of metal that were stacked together the way pages are in a book.

Clockwork Springs

You have to wind up some old clocks with a key. The key winds up a **spiral** spring inside the clock. As the wound-up spring slowly unwinds, it turns the clock hands.

spiral spring

key

The inside of a clock

Clockwork toys use clock springs to make them move. The clock spring turns a **motor**. In the past, many wonderful toys were powered by clockwork motors. Today, most moving toys have electric motors that are powered by **batteries**.

FACT FILE A wind-up radio!

In 1994 Trevor Baylis invented a clockwork radio that does not need batteries. A clockwork motor turns a tiny machine called a dynamo. The dynamo makes electricity. You can wind up the radio when you want to listen.

Pinballs and Cannonballs

A spring fires the steel balls in a pinball machine. When you pull back the plunger, it squeezes the spring. When you let go, the plunger springs forward and pushes the ball up the table.

Human cannonballs are popular acts at the circus. Although it looks as if the clown is fired from a gun by **gunpowder**, this is only the flash of a firework. It is really a big spring inside the cannon that pushes the clown up into the air.

Stapling springs

A staple gun has a strong spring inside. When you squeeze the handle, you squeze the spring. Then, a catch releases the spring, and the gun fires a staple to stick your poster to the wall.

Activities

Making a spring

1. You need a piece of thin wire about 10 inches (25 centimeters) long.
2. Wind the wire around a pencil in a **spiral**.

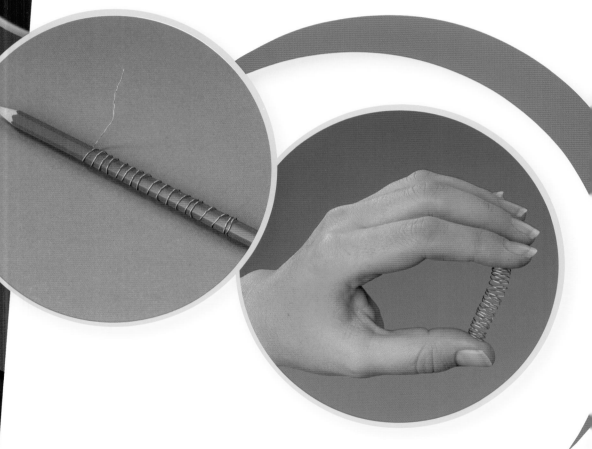

3. Remove the pencil. Now, you have a spring.
4. Squeeze the top and bottom of the spring gently and let go. What happens?

See page 4 to find out more about this.

Measuring weight

1. Measure the length of the spring you have just made.
2. Tie a thread around the middle of a piece of wood.
3. Tie a loop at the other end of the thread.

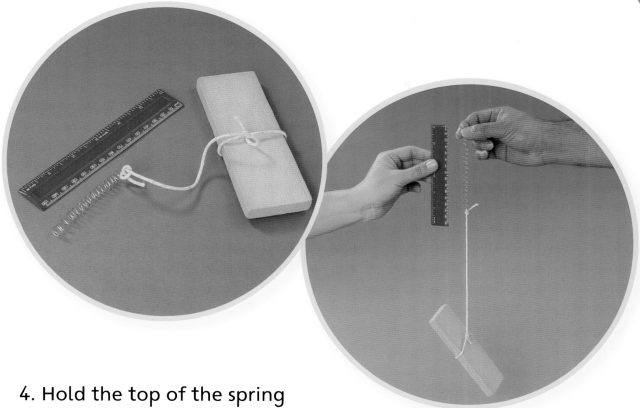

4. Hold the top of the spring and hook the thread to the other end.
5. Measure the length of the spring now that the piece of wood is hanging from it.

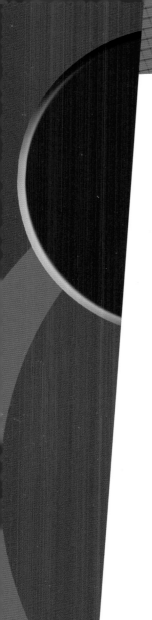

Glossary

battery   small package of chemicals that makes electricity

catch   piece of material that works with a spring to keep an object open or closed

compressed   when something is squeezed or crushed

dial   part of a weighing machine where a pointer moves along a row of numbers to show you the weight

dynamo   machine that makes electricity

forks   pair of rods or arms that hold the front wheel of a bicycle

gunpowder   powdered chemicals that burn with a flash and a bang

lever   rod or a bar that turns around a hinge or pivot

magnify   to make bigger

motocross bike   motorcycle for racing over rough ground

motor   machine that uses electricity or fuels (such as gasoline or coal) to make things move

spiral   special shape that goes along and around at the same time. A corkscrew is a spiral shape.

spring loaded   held in place by a spring

tension   when something is being pulled or stretched

work   energy you use to move something or wind something up

Index